Short Poems
of
Walt Whitman

Selected by C.P. Harrison

Cover Design by 5six Graphics

Walt Whitman Illustration by APCH

A Saturn Fence Publication 2017

Library of Congress Cataloging-in-Publication Data

Harrison, C.P., 1969-
Selected Short Poems of Walt Whitman:
poetry/collection
p. cm.
1.Whitman, Walt 1819-1892 2.Poetry-American.I.Title.

ISBN: 0-9988808-2-5
ISBN-13: 978-0-9988808-2-2

For Jessica and Aidan

CONTENTS

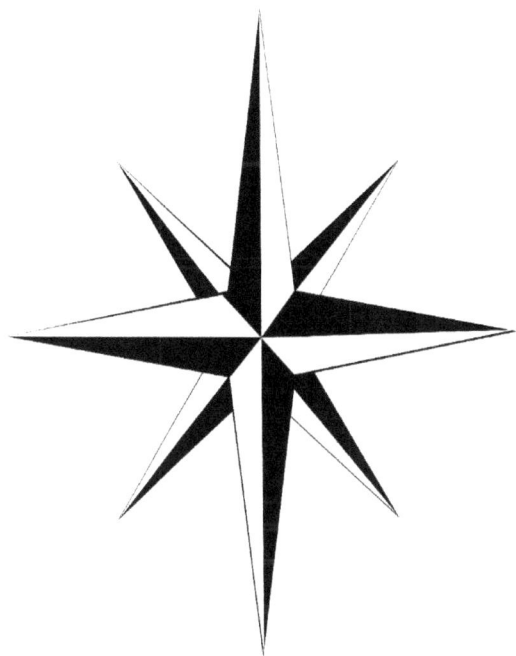

ACKNOWLEDGMENTS

This collection would not have been possible without the guidance and groundwork of all that have contributed to The Walt Whitman Archive under the direction of Kenneth M. Price at the University of Nebraska–Lincoln and Ed Folsom University of Iowa, without the pioneering scholarship of the late Paul Zweig, or the early inspiration of Tom Schulman and Robin Williams. I extend my sincerest gratitude to them all.

Introduction

The collection of poetry you hold in your hand exist, in short, because previously it had not. Those of us with even a passing familiarity with Walt Whitman's poetry, often via a High School English Class, know he is not best remembered for his brevity. We tend to think of the father of American Poetry's all-inclusive grandness, his most well-known poem, *Song of Myself*, being over 1300 lines. We remember "The Good Gray Poet" as being prone to overstate, to catalog, to attempt to tag everything on God's green earth with a blue ribbon. And rightly so, as it is with length and time and space that the American arias of Walt Whitman often soar to their greatest heights.

Checking in with the Whitman canon recently, as one is want to do, it was with surprise that I was reminded how many smaller, stand-alone poems actually exist. Some seem little more than thoughts, a few even titled as such. Many stand out for their "moderness." Notes to self, from minute remembrances to reminders of our grandness. So many of which are a single line or two, verging on haiku. Knowing that the Master's work had been collected and edited ad nauseam, I set out to find a collection of just these smaller pieces. None yet existed, however, and that is where I chose my task.

The task proved to be not without complication. It can certainly be debated, with pride and preference, what constitutes a "short poem." Some may disagree with my selections or omissions. Favorites may have fallen by the wayside. Often, however, it came down to what fit best to tell the tale. That was my true task.

I found that each of these shorter poems can stand rightly on their own. They just as easily expose an arc of their own when read front to back and I've hoped to arrange them as such. They reveal a Whitmanian journey through a lifetime, a day, or even a single thought. A sort of psalms for Walt Whitman's great secular religion of Americanism.

As there is abundant evidence that Whitman was constantly eyeing perfection (he published 6 different versions of the book *Leaves of Grass* over a 27-year span) it was my duty as editor to tread lightly. When in doubt of form or format I've referenced the hand-written originals where available and first editions when possible, with the aid of the Walt Whitman Archive. Barring all else, however, I have erred on the side of literary tradition.

Walt Whitman would be pleased to know that his poetry is still of interest in the 21st century. I hope you find pleasure in his smaller poems, maybe seen in a new light or breathing unencumbered with renewed life.

C.P.Harrison
September 2017

THOU READER

Thou reader throbbest life and pride and love
the same as I,
Therefore for thee the following chants.

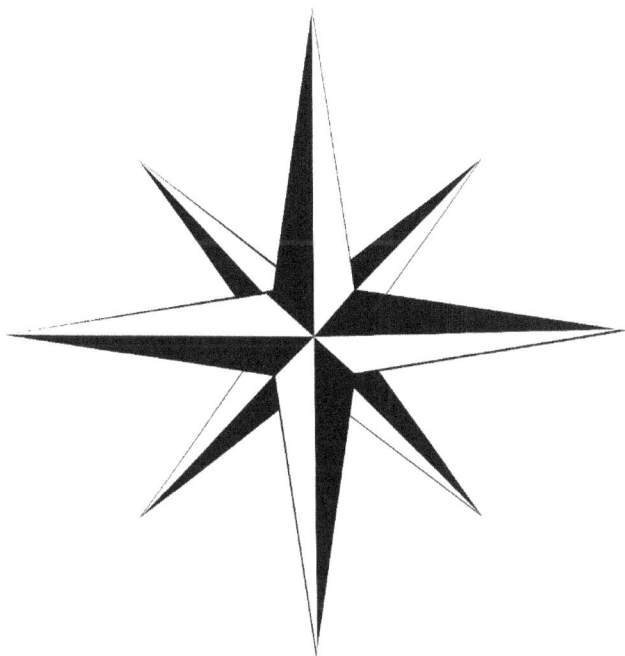

SHUT NOT YOUR DOORS

Shut not your doors to me proud libraries,
For that which was lacking on all your well-fill'd shelves, yet
needed most,
I bring,
Forth from the war emerging, a book I have made,
The words of my book nothing, the drift of it every thing,
A book separate, not link'd with the rest nor felt by the intellect,
But you ye untold latencies will thrill to every page.

HERE THE FRAILEST LEAVES OF ME

Here the frailest leaves of me and yet my strongest lasting,
Here I shade and hide my thoughts, I myself do not expose them,
And yet they expose me more than all my other poems.

WHAT AM I AFTER ALL

What am I after all but a child, pleas'd with the sound of my own name? repeating it over and over;
I stand apart to hear—it never tires me.

To you your name also;
Did you think there was nothing but two or three pronunciations in the sound of your name?

BEGINNING MY STUDIES

Beginning my studies the first step pleas'd me so much,
The mere fact consciousness, these forms, the power of motion,
The least insect or animal, the senses, eyesight, love,
The first step I say awed me and pleas'd me so much,
I have hardly gone and hardly wish'd to go any farther,
But stop and loiter all the time to sing it in ecstatic songs.

TO YOU

Let us twain walk aside from the rest;
Now we are together privately, do you discard
ceremony,
Come! vouchsafe to me what has yet been vouchsafed
to none—Tell me the whole story,
Tell me what you would not tell your brother, wife,
husband, or physician.

THESE CAROLS

These carols sung to cheer my passage through the world I see,
For completion I dedicate to the Invisible World.

GLIDING O'ER ALL

Gliding o'er all, through all,
Through Nature, Time, and Space,
As a ship on the waters advancing,
The voyage of the soul—not life alone,
Death, many deaths I'll sing.

STRONGER LESSONS

Have you learned lessons only of those who admired
you, and were tender with you, and stood aside
for you?
Have you not learned the great lessons of those who
rejected you, and braced themselves against
you? or who treated you with contempt, or
disputed the passage with you?

LIFE AND DEATH

The two old, simple problems ever intertwined,
Close home, elusive, present, baffled, grappled.
By each successive age insoluble, pass'd on,
To ours to-day—and we pass on the same.

LIFE

Ever the undiscouraged, resolute, struggling soul of man;
(Have former armies fail'd? then we send fresh armies—and
fresh again;)
Ever the grappled mystery of all earth's ages old or new;
Ever the eager eyes, hurrahs, the welcome-clapping hands, the
loud applause;
Ever the soul dissatisfied, curious, unconvinced at last;
Struggling to-day the same—battling the same.

LESSONS

There are who teach only the sweet lessons of peace and safety;
But I teach lessons of war and death to those I love,
That they readily meet invasions, when they come.

THIS DAY, O SOUL

This day, O soul, I give you a wondrous mirror;
Long in the dark, in tarnish and cloud it lay—But the cloud
has pass'd, and the tarnish gone;
…Behold, O soul! it is now a clean and bright mirror,
Faithfully showing you all the things of the world.

THE UNTOLD WANT

The untold want by life and land ne'er granted,
Now voyager sail thou forth to seek and find.

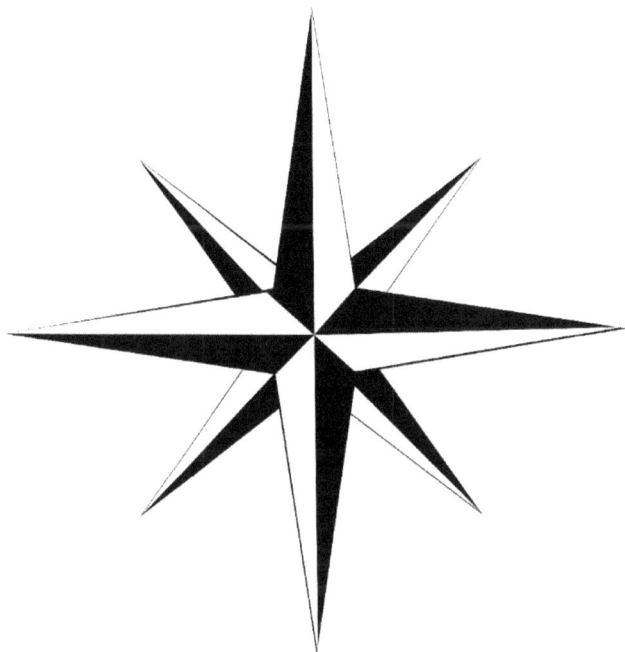

OUT OF MAY'S SHOWS SELECTED

Apple orchards, the trees all cover'd with blossoms;
Wheat fields carpeted far and near in vital emerald green;
The eternal, exhaustless freshness of each early morning;
The yellow, golden, transparent haze of the warm afternoon sun;
The aspiring lilac bushes with profuse purple or white flowers.

TO YOU

Stranger! if you, passing, meet me, and desire to
speak to me, why should you not speak to me?
And why should I not speak to you?

OFFERINGS

A thousand perfect men and women appear,
Around each gathers a cluster of friends, and gay children and
youths, with offerings.

LOCATIONS AND TIMES

Locations and times—what is it in me that meets them all,
whenever and wherever,
and makes me at home?
Forms, colors, densities, odors—what is it in me that corresponds
with them?

THE FIRST DANDELION

Simple and fresh and fair from winter's close
emerging,
As if no artifice of fashion, business, politics,
had ever been,
Forth from its sunny nook of shelter'd grass—
innocent, golden, calm as the dawn,
The spring's first dandelion shows its trustful
face.

A FARM PICTURE

Through the ample open door of the peaceful country barn,
A sunlit pasture field with cattle and horses feeding,
And haze and vista, and the far horizon fading away.

THOUGHT

Of obedience, faith, adhesiveness;
As I stand aloof and look there is to me something profoundly
affecting in large masses of men following the lead of those
who do not believe in men.

TO A WESTERN BOY

Many things to absorb I teach to help you become eleve of mine;
Yet if blood like mine circle not in your veins,
If you be not silently selected by lovers and do not silently select
lovers,
Of what use is it that you seek to become eleve of mine?

A PRAIRIE SUNSET

Shot gold, maroon and violet, dazzling silver, emerald, fawn,
The earth's whole amplitude and nature's multiform power
consigned for once to colors;
The light, the genial air possessed by them—
colors till now unknown,
No limit, confine—not the Western sky alone—
the high meridian—North, South, all,
Pure luminous color fighting the silent shadows to the last.

BEAUTIFUL WOMEN

Women sit, or move to and fro—some old, some young;
The young are beautiful—but the old are more beautiful than the
young.

AFTER THE ARGUMENT

A group of little children with their ways and chatter flow in,
Like welcome rippling water o'er my heated nerves and flesh.

MOTHER AND BABE

I see the sleeping babe, nestling the breast of its mother;
The sleeping mother and babe—hush'd, I study them
long and long

THE TORCH

On my Northwest coast in the midst of the night a fishermen's
group stands watching,
Out on the lake that expands before them, others are spearing
salmon,
The canoe, a dim shadowy thing, moves across the black water,
Bearing a torch ablaze at the prow.

THE COMMONPLACE

The commonplace I sing;
How cheap is health! how cheap nobility!
Abstinence, no falsehood, no gluttony, lust;
The open air I sing, freedom, toleration,
(Take here the mainest lesson—less from books—less from the
schools,)
The common day and night—the common earth and waters,
Your farm—your work, trade, occupation,
The democratic wisdom underneath, like solid ground for all.

THOUGHT

Of Equality—as if it harm'd me, giving others the same chances
and rights as myself—as if it were not indispensable to
my own rights that others possess the same.

THIS MOMENT YEARNING AND THOUGHTFUL

This moment yearning and thoughtful sitting alone,
It seems to me there are other men in other lands yearning and
thoughtful,
It seems to me I can look over and behold them in Germany,
Italy, France, Spain,
Or far, far away, in China, or in Russia or Japan, talking other
dialects,
And it seems to me if I could know those men I should become
attached to them as I do to men in my own lands,
O I know we should be brethren and lovers,
I know I should be happy with them.

TRANSPOSITIONS

Let the reformers descend from the stands
where they are forever
bawling—let an idiot or insane person appear
on each of the stands;
Let judges and criminals be transposed—let the prison-
keepers be put in prison—let those that were prisoners take
the keys;
Let them that distrust birth and death lead the rest.

THE RUNNER

On a flat road runs the well-train'd runner;
He is lean and sinewy, with muscular legs;
He is thinly clothed—he leans forward as he runs,
With lightly closed fists, and arms partially rais'd.

HAST NEVER COME TO THEE AN HOUR

Hast never come to thee an hour,
A sudden gleam divine, precipitating, bursting all these bubbles,
fashions, wealth?
These eager business aims—books, politics, art, amours,
To utter nothingness?

MANNAHATTA

My city's fit and noble name resumed,
Choice aboriginal name, with marvellous beauty, meaning,
A rocky founded island—shores where ever gayly dash the coming,
going, hurrying sea waves.

YEAR THAT TREMBLED AND REEL'D BENEATH ME

Year that trembled and reel'd beneath me!
Your summer wind was warm enough—yet the air I
breathed froze me;
A thick gloom fell through the sunshine
and darken'd me;
Must I change my triumphant songs? said I to myself;
Must I indeed learn to chant the cold dirges of the baffled?
And sullen hymns of defeat?

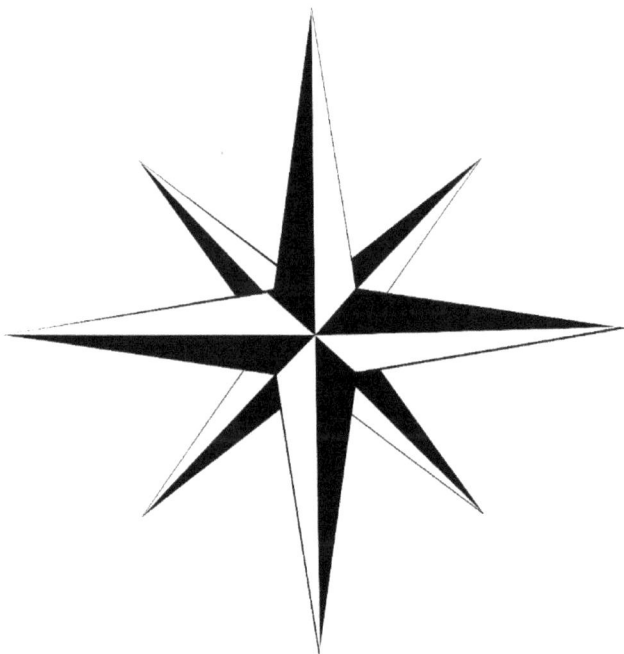

ASHES OF SOLDIERS: EPIGRAPH

Again a verse for sake of you,
You soldiers in the ranks — you Volunteers,
Who bravely fighting, silent fell,
To fill unmention'd graves.

LONG, TOO LONG AMERICA

Long, too long America,
Traveling roads all even and peaceful you learn'd from joys
and prosperity only,
But now, ah now, to learn from crises of anguish,
advancing, grappling with direst fate and recoiling not,
And now to conceive and show to the world what your
children en-masse really are,
(For who except myself has yet conceiv'd what your
children en-masse really are?)

I HEAR IT WAS CHARGED AGAINST ME

I hear it was charged against me that I sought to
destroy institutions;
But really I am neither for nor against institutions;
(What indeed have I in common with them?—Or
what with the destruction of them?)
Only I will establish in the Mannahatta, and in every
city of These States, inland and seaboard,
And in the fields and woods, and above every keel
little or large, that dents the water,
Without edifices, or rules, or trustees, or any argument,
The institution of the dear love of comrades.

FOR HIM I SING

For him I sing,
I raise the present on the past,
(As some perennial tree out of its roots, the present on the past,)
With time and space I him dilate and fuse the immortal laws,
To make himself by them the law unto himself.

TO THE EAST AND TO THE WEST

To the East and to the West;
To the man of the Seaside State, and of Pennsylvania,
To the Kanadian of the North—to the Southerner I
love;
These, with perfect trust, to depict you as myself—
the germs are in all men;
I believe the main purport of These States is to found
a superb friendship, exalté, previously unknown,
Because I perceive it waits, and has been always waiting,
latent in all men.

FROM MONTAUK POINT

I stand as on some mighty eagle's beak,
Eastward the sea absorbing, viewing,
(nothing but sea and sky,)
The tossing waves, the foam, the ships in the distance,
The wild unrest, the snowy, curling caps—that inbound urge
and urge of waves,
Seeking the shores forever.

THE SHIP STARTING

Lo, the unbounded sea,
On its breast a ship starting, spreading all sails, carrying even her
moonsails,
The pennant is flying aloft as she speeds she speeds so stately—
below emulous waves press forward,
They surround the ship with shining curving motions and foam.

TO A PRESIDENT

All you are doing and saying is to America dangled
mirages,
You have not learned of Nature—of the politics of
Nature, you have not learned the great amplitude,
rectitude, impartiality,
You have not seen that only such as they are for
These States,
And that what is less than they, must sooner or later
lift off from These States.

TO THE STATES

To the States or any one of them, or any city of the States,
Resist much, obey little,
Once unquestioning obedience, once fully enslaved,
Once fully enslaved, no nation, state, city of this earth, ever afterward resumes its liberty.

LEAFLETS

What General has a good army in himself, has a good army;
He happy in himself, or she happy in herself, is happy.

WORLD, TAKE GOOD NOTICE

World, take good notice, silver stars fading,
Milky hue ript, weft of white detaching,
Coals thirty-six, baleful and burning,
Scarlet, significant, hands off warning,
Now and henceforth flaunt from these shores.

I DREAM'D IN A DREAM

I dream'd in a dream I saw a city invincible to the attacks of the whole of the rest of the earth,
I dream'd that was the new city of Friends,
Nothing was greater there than the quality of robust love, it led the rest,
It was seen every hour in the actions of the men of that city,
And in all their looks and words.

THIS DUST WAS ONCE THE MAN

This dust was once the man,
Gentle, plain, just and resolute, under whose cautious hand,
Against the foulest crime in history known in any land or age,
Was saved the Union of these States.

THOU WEST THAT GAVE'ST HIM TO US

That rear'dst him on ample prairies,
and on the breasts of thy, fresh,
rivers; This day we return to thee bearing his body.

STILL THOUGH THE ONE I SING

Still though the one I sing,
(One, yet of contradictions made,) I dedicate to Nationality,
I leave in him revolt, (O latent right of insurrection! O quench-
less, indispensable fire!)

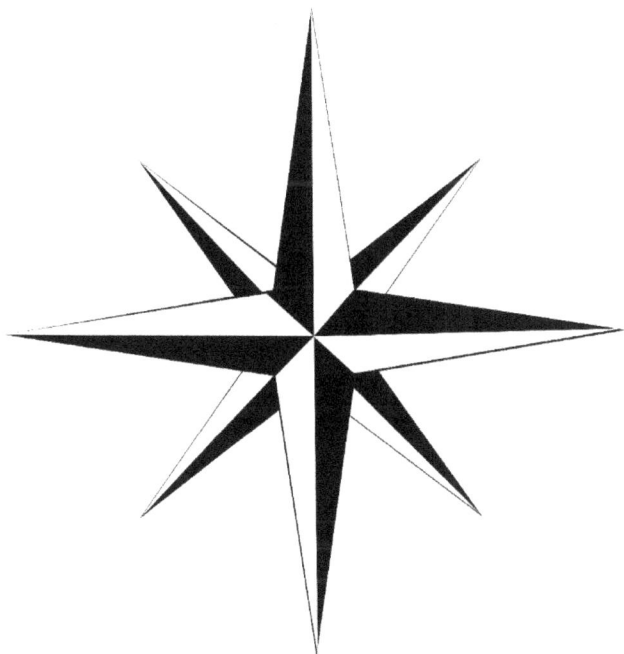

OTHERS MAY PRAISE WHAT THEY LIKE

Others may praise what they like;
But I, from the banks of the running Missouri, praise
       nothing, in art, or aught else,
Till it has breathed well the atmosphere of this river—
       also the western prairie-scent,
And fully exudes it again.

SOMETIMES WITH ONE I LOVE

Sometimes with one I love, I fill myself with rage, for
fear I effuse unreturn'd love;
But now I think there is no unreturn'd love—the pay
is certain, one way or another;
(I loved a certain person ardently, and my love
was not return'd;
Yet out of that, I have written these songs.)

THAT SHADOW MY LIKENESS

That shadow my likeness that goes to and fro seeking a
livelihood,
chattering, chaffering,
How often I find myself standing and looking at it where it
flits,
How often I question and doubt whether that is really me;
But among my lovers and caroling these songs,
O I never doubt whether that is really me.

AS ADAM EARLY IN THE MORNING

As Adam early in the morning,
Walking forth from the bower refresh'd with sleep,
Behold me where I pass, hear my voice, approach,
Touch me, touch the palm of your hand to my body as I pass,
Be not afraid of my body.

I AM HE THAT ACHES WITH LOVE

I am he that aches with amorous love;
Does the earth gravitate? does not all matter, aching,   attract all
matter?
So the body of me to all I meet or know.

PERFECTIONS

Only themselves understand themselves, and the like
of themselves,
As Souls only understand Souls.

THOUGHT

Of Justice—as if Justice could be any thing but the same ample
law, expounded by natural judges and saviors,
As if it might be this thing or that thing, according to decisions.

A CHILD'S AMAZE

Silent and amazed, even when a little boy,
I remember I heard the preacher every Sunday put God
in his statements,
As contending against some being or influence.

NOT MY ENEMIES EVER INVADE ME

Not my enemies ever invade me—no harm to my pride from
them I fear;
But the lovers I recklessly love—lo! how they master me!
Lo! me, ever open and helpless, bereft of my strength!
Utterly abject, grovelling on the ground before them.

O YOU WHOM I OFTEN AND SILENTLY COME

O you whom I often and silently come where you are that I may
be with you,
As I walk by your side or sit near, or remain in the same room
with you,
Little you know the subtle electric fire that for your sake is playing
within me.

AFTER THE DAZZLE OF DAY

After the dazzle of day is gone,
Only the dark, dark night shows to my eyes the stars;
After the clangor of organ majestic, or chorus, or perfect band,
Silent, athwart my soul, moves the symphony true.

VISOR'D

A mask, a perpetual natural disguiser of herself,
Concealing her face, concealing her form,
Changes and transformations every hour, every moment,
Falling upon her even when she sleeps.

LOOK DOWN FAIR MOON

Look down, fair moon, and bathe this scene;
Pour softly down night's nimbus floods, on faces ghastly, swollen, purple;
On the dead, on their backs, with their arms toss'd wide,
Pour down your unstinted nimbus, sacred moon.

A CLEAR MIDNIGHT

This is thy hour O Soul, thy free flight into the wordless,
Away from books, away from art, the day erased, the lesson done,
Thee fully forth emerging, silent, gazing, pondering the themes
thou lovest best,
Night, sleep, death and the stars.

THEN LAST OF ALL

Then last of all, caught from these shores, this hill,
Of you O tides, the mystic human meaning:
Only by law of you, your swell and ebb, enclosing me the same,
The brain that shapes, the voice that chants this song.

THE CALMING THOUGHT OF ALL

That coursing on, whate'er men's speculations,
Amid the changing schools, theologies, philosophies,
Amid the bawling presentations new and old,
The round earth's silent vital laws, facts, modes continue.

OF MANY A SMUTCH'D DEED REMINISCENT

Full of wickedness, I—of many a smutch'd deed reminiscent—
of worse deeds capable,
Yet I look composedly upon nature, drink day and night the joys
of life, and await death with perfect equanimity,
Because of my tender and boundless love for him I love and
because of his boundless love for me.

AS IN A SWOON

As in a swoon, one instant,
Another sun, ineffable, full-dazzles
me,
And all the orbs I knew, with
brighter, unknown orbs, ten thousand fold,
One instant of the future land—
Heaven's land.

SOLID, IRONICAL, ROLLING ORB

Solid, ironical, rolling orb!
Master of all, and matter of fact!—at last I accept your
terms;
Bringing to practical, vulgar tests, of all my ideal
dreams,
And of me, as lover and hero.

THEN SHALL PERCEIVE

In softness, languor, bloom, and growth,
Thine eyes, ears, all thy sense — thy loftiest attribute — all that
takes cognizance of beauty,
Shall rouse and fill — then shall perceive!

ONE THOUGHT EVER AT THE FORE

One thought ever at the fore -
That in the Divine Ship, the World, breasting Time and Space,
All Peoples of the globe together sail, sail the same voyage,
Are bound to the same destination.

ROAMING IN THOUGHT

(*After reading* Hegel)

Roaming in thought over the Universe, I saw the little that is
Good steadily hastening towards immortality,
And the vast all that is call'd Evil I saw hastening to merge itself
and become lost and dead.

AFTER AN INTERVAL

(Nov. 22,1875 Midnight- Saturn and Mars in Conjunction)

After an interval, reading, here in the midnight,
With the great stars looking on—all the stars of Orion looking,
And the silent Pleiades—and the duo looking of Saturn and ruddy
Mars;
Pondering, reading my own songs, after a long interval, (sorrow and
death familiar now)
Ere closing the book, what pride! what joy! to find them
Standing so well the test of death and night,
And the duo of Saturn and Mars!

.

TWILIGHT

The soft voluptuous opiate shades,
The sun just gone, the eager light dispell'd—(I too will soon be gone, dispell'd,)
A haze—nirwana—rest and night—oblivion.

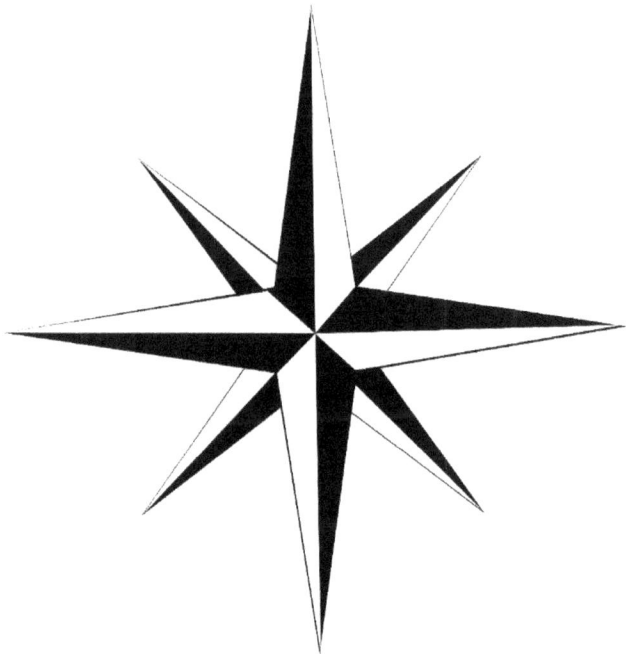

JOY, SHIPMATE, JOY!

Joy, shipmate, joy!
(Pleas'd to my soul at death I cry,)
Our life is closed, our life begins,
The long, long anchorage we leave,
The ship is clear at last, she leaps!
She swiftly courses from the shore,
Joy, shipmate, joy.

THE FEW DROPS KNOWN

Of heroes, history, grand events, premises, myths, poems,
The few drops known must stand for oceans of the unknown,
On this beautiful and thick peopl'd earth, here and there a little
specimen put on record.
A little of Greeks and Romans, a few Hebrew canticles, a few
death odors as from graves, from Egypt—
What are they to the long and copious retrospect of antiquity

FOR US TWO, READER DEAR

Simple, spontaneous, curious, two souls interchanging,
With the original testimony for us continued to the last.

YOUTH, DAY, OLD AGE AND NIGHT

Youth, large, lusty, loving—youth full of grace, force, fascination,
Do you know that Old Age may come after you with equal grace,
force, fascination?

Day full-blown and splendid—day of the immense sun, action,
ambition, laughter,
The Night follows close with millions of suns, and sleep and
restoring darkness.

O LIVING ALWAYS, ALWAYS DYING

O living always, always dying!
O the burials of me past and present,
O me while I stride ahead, material, visible, imperious as ever;
O me, what I was for years, now dead, (I lament not, I am content;)
O to disengage myself from those corpses of me, which I turn and look at where I cast them,
To pass on, (O living! always living!) and leave the corpses behind.

TO OLD AGE

I see in you the estuary that enlarges and spreads itself grandly as it pours in the great sea.

MEMORIES

How sweet the silent backward tracings!
The wanderings as in dreams—the meditation of old times
resumed—their loves, joys, persons, voyages.

THE DISMANTLED SHIP

In some unused lagoon, some nameless bay,
On sluggish, lonesome waters, anchor'd near the shore,
An old, dismasted, gray and batter'd ship, disabled, done,
After free voyages to all the seas of earth, haul'd up at last and
hawser'd tight,
Lies rusting, mouldering.

AS I SIT WRITING HERE

As I sit writing here, sick and grown old,
Not my least burden is that dulness of the years, querilities,
Ungracious glooms, aches, lethargy, constipation, whimpering
ennui,
May filter in my daily songs

AND YET NOT YOU ALONE

And yet not you alone, twilight and burying ebb,
Nor you, ye lost designs alone—nor failures, aspirations;
I know, divine deceitful ones, your glamour's seeming,
Duly by you, by you alone, the tide and light again—duly
the hinges turning,
Duly the needed discord-parts offsetting, blending,
Weaving from you, from Sleep, Night, Death itself,

The rhythmus of Birth eternal.

AN EVENING LULL

After a week of physical anguish,
Unrest and pain, and feverish heat,
Toward the ending day a calm and lull comes on,
Three hours of peace and soothing rest of brain

LINGERING LAST DROPS

And whence and why come you?
We know not whence, (was the answer,)
We only know that we drift here with the rest,
That we linger'd and lagg'd—but were wafted at last, and are
now here,
To make the passing shower's concluding drops.

PORTALS

What are those of the known but to ascend
and enter the Unknown?
And what are those of life but for Death?

PENSIVE AND FALTERING

Pensive and faltering,
The words *the Dead* I write,
For living are the Dead,
(Haply the only living, only real,
And I the apparition, I the spectre.)

AN ENDED DAY

The soothing sanity and blitheness of completion,
The pomp and hurried contest-glare and rush are done;
Now triumph! transformation! jubilate!

THE BEAUTY OF THE SHIP

When, staunchly entering port,
After long ventures, hauling up, worn and old,
Better'd by sea and wind, torn by many a fight,
With the original sails all gone, replaced, or mended,
I only saw, at last the beauty of the ship.

LONG, LONG HENCE

After a long, long course, hundreds of years, denials,
Accumulations, rous'd love and joy and thought,
Hopes, wishes, aspirations, ponderings, victories, myriads of
readers,
Coating, compassing, covering—after ages' and ages'
encrustations,
Then only may these songs reach fruition.

FROM MY LAST YEARS

From my last years, last thoughts I here bequeath,
Scatter'd and dropt, in seeds, and wafted to the West,
Through moisture of Ohio, prairie soil of Illinois—through
Colorado, California air,
For Time to germinate fully.

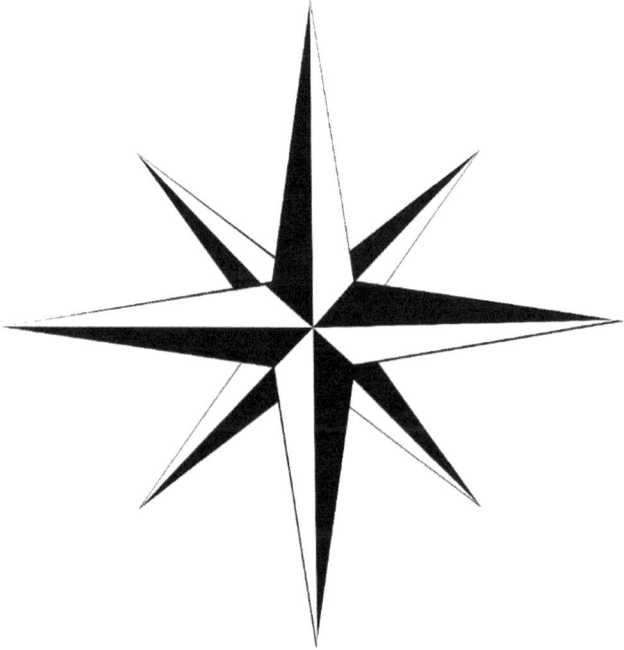

TO THE READER AT PARTING

Now, dearest comrade, lift me to your face,
We must separate awhile—Here! take from my lips this kiss.
Whoever you are, I give it especially to you;
So long!—And I hope we shall meet again.

Suggested Reading

Kinnell, Galway, *The Essential Whitman*

Roggenbuck, Steve, *I Love You, Before Long I Die (A Walt Whitman Mixtape)*

Williams, C.K., *On Whitman*

Zweig, Paul, *Walt Whitman The Making of the Poet*

About the Editor

C.P.Harrison is a poet whose other books include *One Hundred Flarf-Ku* (2014), *Every Word You Ever Heard* (2015) and the forthcoming *America: An Autobiography*. He lives in Austin, Texas with his family.

Please support
www.whitmanarchive.org